THE BIGGEST BLUFF

How I Learned To Pay Attention,

Master Myself, And Win By Maria

Konnikova

Summary

Book Summary Description

How much of life can be found in the game of poker? After a series of unfortunate events in her family, psychologist Maria Konnikova decides to enter the world of poker and eventually tries to compete in the World Series of Poker Main Event or WSOP, to determine how much of *chance* and *luck* she could actually control. She spends almost a whole year gearing up for the WSOP and ends up meeting a number of poker greats, facing many ups and downs, and playing countless tournaments in an effort to hone her skills fast enough to have a chance at winning the Main Event. More than poker, this book is about taking control of one's life, improving decision making skills, and learning to maximize the limited information presented to us in everyday situations. It's an analysis of human behavior, seen through the lens of poker hands, bad beats, and bluffs.

Table of Contents

Trivia Questions About This Book

1. How many chapters are in the book?

2. How did Maria Konnikova, the author, get interested in poker?

3. Who was her poker coach?

4. What was his coach's main advice to her?

5. Where did Konnikova first start to play poker?

6. What kind of poker did Konnikova choose to play?

7. Who are the other poker players that coached Konnikova?

8. In what chapter does the author cite Immanuel Kant's Critique of Pure Reason?

9. What is 'bankroll'?

10. What is a 'chop'?

11. What is 'tilt'?

12. When was the book published?

13. What genre does the book fall under?

Trivia Questions About Maria Konnikova

1. What is her original profession?

2. Where did she get her degree and what degree/s does she have?

3. Where did she get her PhD?

4. What was the recurring illness that she has?

5. What was the author's online poker username?

SUMMARY

Maria Konnikova's The Biggest Bluff - How I Learned to Pay Attention, Master Myself, and Win is about the author's journey to understand how to take control of her life through the game of poker. The book was originally published last June 23, 2020 and falls under the self-help genre. Konnikova is a psychologist and a writer. She has a bachelor's degree in psychology and creative writing from Harvard University, as well as a PhD in psychology from Columbia University.

The book is divided into 16 chapters in total, with each chapter's title including the place and time at one particular moment of Konnikova's poker journey. The order is not necessarily chronological, but Konnikova arranges her story in such a way to forward her ideas and learnings about the relationship of poker in contrast to life. Her background as a psychologist and a member of the academe is reflected in the way she writes her story. Aside from the numerous anecdotes she has in her poker journey, each idea or concept she forwards is backed with data, literature, and scientific studies.

1. A Prelude

The first chapter is aptly named *A Prelude - Las Vegas, July 2017*. Here, we find the author in the biggest poker tournament in the world—the Main Event of the World Series of Poker (WSOP). She describes one of the poker tables in the tourney with eight seats and one chair empty. It is revealed that this was her chair and her chips were dwindling fast as moments go by that she wasn't playing. At this moment, Konnikova is in the fetal position in one of the bathrooms of the Rio Hotel and Casino, contemplating why she was in a particular state. She asks herself if it could be food poisoning, stress, stomach flu, or her life-long battle of having migraines. Whatever it was, she emphasized that no matter how much man plans, "God laughs." After prepping endlessly and planning for all contingencies, she says that some things in life are "stubbornly outside your control."

In the prelude, Konnikova outlines why she decided to get into poker. One of her main motivations in trying her hand with the game was to better understand the line between luck and skill. She wanted to learn about what she could control and what she couldn't. And as a foreshadowing of things to come, she says that one of the things she learned throughout this journey was that you *cannot bluff chance*. Throughout the book, poker is often compared to dealing with *chance* in real life. Konnikova double's down on this concept early on as she says the *Why* does not matter in Poker—her hands were still being dealt regardless of her being nauseous and vomiting in a hotel bathroom. Life doesn't care and dealing with this fact is one of the central themes of the book.

To end the prelude, we're introduced to Erik Seidel as her poker coach. He sends Konnikova a text asking how she was in the WSOP, to which she replies that she was fine. He wishes her luck and she says that she needed exactly that—luck.

2. Ante Up

The next chapter is entitled Ante Up - New York, Late Summer, 2016. In this chapter, Erik Seidel is given the spotlight. The author describes Seidel as the most self-effacing poker champion there was in the world. He was a standout, not only for his skills, but for longevity. The author stressed how amazing it was for Erik to last in the poker game, starting out in the late eighties, and still contending for number one in rankings. She says that despite predictions of Erik's decline due to his 'dated' style of play, which was a psychological approach in contrast to the more mathematical way being taken by new players, Erik still stayed on top. The author shares that she had also asked Erik the inevitable question of finding out what the secret to his success was, to which he said, "pay attention." She explained that these two words were things we ignored more often than not in our daily lives, as presence in the moment was far more difficult than "the path of least resistance".

In this chapter, the author tells us a little about her story as a child, where she says she had "perhaps the greatest luck of my life" as her parents left the Soviet Union when she was younger and she was the first person in her family to make it in college in the United States. She asks, "how often are we actually in control?", referring to control in our lives. According to her and the studies she made during her doctoral research, people tend to overestimate their own skill relative to luck or chance. They overestimated the degree of control they had over events in their lives and because of this, their decision-making skills deteriorated. She urged that people should train themselves to see the world in a probabilistic light. However, she claimed that no matter how many charts or data you'd show people, they would stick to their gut according to their view of what was happening unless themselves were in the same experience before they knew somebody else that did. Here she stresses that experiences are incredibly skewed. Konnikova says that they may teach us things about life, but they don't teach us well.

The next section of the chapter talks about the author in the year 2015. According to her, this was not a good year for her family. In the first week of January, her mother lost her job where she worked for almost 20 years. After a few months, her grandmother died in a tragic slipping accident, falling on a metal bed frame. Lastly, her husband lost his job as his startup company did not pan out. After these negative events in her life, the author shares that she retreated to reading as her way to understand what was happening. This would be the first time in a while that she needed to support her family financially as a freelance writer.

The author shares that she had come across John von Neumman's Theory of Games and Economic Behavior, which is where she found a fascination for poker. In the book, he explained that he loved poker for the balance it had between skill and chance, which for him, governed life. Here, the author explains that in her foray into the poker world, she chose Texas Hold'em as her poker game of choice because it had a useful balance between skill and chance and because it had no limits in how much you could bet. These were two things that the author found to be a particularly strong metaphor for daily decision making.

The author then returns to her first meeting with Seidel. She explains his resume as a professional player: having 8 WSOP bracelets, being a Poker Hall of Fame member, boasting the fourth-highest tournament career winnings, and having a World Poker Tour Title. The author tells us that the reason why Erik Seidel took up her offer to be her coach was because she was a psychologist. He said that this would be a big help in poker and that she was approaching the game from "the area of most value," with newer players being very math-based.

The last part of the chapter finds the author saying that this endeavor was only supposed to be one year. But it turned into a new life. Here she reveals that she eventually became a champion. From an amateur poker player, she became a professional. She ends the chapter telling readers that poker teaches us how and when we can take true control, deal with elements of pure luck, and being more observant to our surroundings. She says that this book is not about how to play poker, but about how to play the world.

3. The Birth of a Gambler

The next chapter is entitled *The Birth of a Gambler*, where we find the author in Boston, in the fall of 2016. Konnikova shares the story of how she had shared her plan of going into poker with her grandmother during a family visit, and how the elder was not overly impressed with what she would be doing. Her grandmother asks her "You are going to be a gambler?". The author says that no matter her reasoning with her, she would still be considered a "moral degenerate by strangers". Her grandmother had wanted her to continue being a professor. Konnikova described her grandmother's sadness "for the life I'm about to throw away". This exchange highlights one of the author's main points in the chapter, which is that poker itself is full of misconceptions. The first of which is that poker is equivalent to gambling. The author emphasizes that poker players actually gambled less than most people because the game involved more skill than many casino games. Furthermore, she argues that to be a winning player, you had to have superior skill.

At this point, she compares poker players to investors, who she says are regarded as having the more respectable profession. According to the author, investors have a remarkable ability to ignore statistical information in favor of their own intuition. She held that numerous studies have shown that these investors were often better served not trading at all, because of their tendency to follow their intuition instead of listening to the data.

She also argues that because there is money on the line in poker, people tended to make better decisions. She says that "our minds learn when we have a stake, a real stake, in the outcome of learning." She underscores this point by citing Immanuel Kant's Critique of Pure Reason. According to the author, Kant proposed betting as "an antidote" to "false confidence" people had. It was a means to defer seeing black and white, when in fact we should "rightly see gray" as Kant described. The author cited Kant's proposition where he makes use of a doctor as an example. In Kant's situation, a doctor reaches a verdict about a patient's illness. He explains that the doctor's diagnosis is not necessarily correct but that it is merely the best he could conclude given a particular set of information. However, if one were to ask the doctor to bet on his diagnosis, it would happen that the doctor would be startled and pause before making his final verdict. For the author, betting on the uncertain was one of the best ways to curb the usual errors in the way we made decisions. There is personal accountability, without the chance to deflect it to someone else, according to her.

It's in this chapter as well that the author outlines a brief historical lesson about poker's origins. The author explains that the game originated from its earliest form in 1803, with some Frenchmen in Louisiana who were in a slow-moving steamship on the way to New Orleans.

To end the chapter, the author brings us back to her encounter with her grandmother. She explains once again that no matter what she did, her grandmother was "still positive [she was] going over to the dark side". In their last exchange of words, Konnikova describes her annoyance when her grandmother told her that "it's only a game." Konnikova argues against this point by reiterating that poker was the more skilled endeavor to take.

4. The Art of Losing

The next chapter is called *The Art of Losing*, where we find the author in the fall of 2017. In this chapter, the author recounts one of her lessons with Erik Seidel at the Fairway Market Café. The author emphasizes how important finding a good mentor is when it comes to learning a new skill and expounds on how the best mentors know when to delegate their teaching. We're introduced by Konnikova to a second teacher, Dan Harrington. Dan is Erik's longtime friend, back when Erik used to play backgammon. Their background stems from a backgammon game that had Erik, the newcomer, face off with the stalwart that was Dan. Dan eventually won but this game sparked a lifelong friendship, where Erik was able to influence Dan into joining the poker game. The author explains that Dan Harrington is the author of one of the best textbooks on Hold'em, a classic as she described. Therefore, Erik delegated Maria's learning of the game to the person who wrote it's textbook. The author then talks about her first meeting with Dan and shares that while there are poker strategies discussed in their first session, the main talking points they had were on the importance of failure.

Afterwards, Erik determines that Maria has enough knowledge to start playing for real, albeit online. The author describes how she held tight on Dan Harrington's books while she focused on playing online, as there were ten months from the Main Event, and she had yet to play any real-life game of poker.

During one of their lessons, Erik explains to Maria that an important tenet in playing poker is not being hyper aggressive in her style of play. He says that most players that utilize this strategy usually go broke and never last long in a given tournament. Both Dan and Erik emphasize that the best way to succeed is to be solid fundamentally, and then add hyper-aggressiveness in play. However, Konnikova explains that the aggressiveness must be used purposefully, at the right place and the right time.

Dan and Maria continue talking about poker terms, strategies, and how hands play out. In their discussion, Dan underscores that the most important thing in Maria's journey was for her to be defeated. Going back to their topic of failure, Dan explains that Maria will not be able to know if she has what it takes if she doesn't fail. She won't be able to know if she's thinking correctly if she does not get beaten. He quotes Mike Tyson, where he said that "everyone has a plan until you get punched in the mouth." Dan tells Maria that it's crucial that she develops her critical thinking and self-assessment abilities to reevaluate where she is at any point of her career or at any point in a given game. He adds that "you become a big winner when you lose" and Maria agrees, as she continued on to say that losing was what "brought [her] to the table in the first place". She said that "to lose constructively...would help me lose in life, lose and come back.."

The next part of the chapter, the author talks about Erik's origins as a poker player. After losing his job in his early days, with his wife just getting pregnant, Erik was able to overcome these obstacles with his complete lack of ego. Aside from his poker skills, Konnikova explains that Erik learns from losing. He quotes Erik who says that when things go wrong, people see it "as unfairness that's always surrounding them." He adds that people don't take a step back to analyze their own decisions or where they may have gone wrong.

Furthermore, Erik emphasizes that the best way to play poker is to have "less certainty. More inquiry." Konnikova stresses that for Erik, there is no simple answer in knowing what the best hand in poker is. Rather, it's a constant process of inquiry. Konnikova explains that Erik does not give her the specific pair of hands or how to play them because he was being mean. Instead, it's because giving her an answer would deprive her the ability to make a decision. All he can do, according to the author, is to give her the tools, the "building blocks of thoughts". She adds that it is she that would be the one who must find the way through.

5. The Mind of a Strategist

The following chapter is named *The Mind of a Strategist*, set in New York, year 2016, late fall. The author recounts the new morning routine she has developed, where she would take a walk with Erik for a lesson and subsequently enter the world of online poker. Konnikova explains that online poker is the most efficient way to get the kind of practice she needed, without having to go through decades of casino sessions. She says that her continued online poker sessions were her version of the 10,000 hour rule. However, the only problem with her setup is that poker is illegal in her home state of New York because of the 2016 Unlawful Internet Gambling Enforcement Act. Because of this, she had to travel to New Jersey to play online poker, as individual states outside of New York were not barred from legalizing the sport.

The next scene has Maria and Erik together, talking about her online poker profile. Her username is *the psychic*, as it embodied many of the traits she wanted to convey, according to her. Here, Maria takes us through an online game where she mistakenly thought that a jack-ten was a good drawing hand and subsequently lost because of playing it. She explains that her primary consideration from doing so was that Erik had told her that it was a good hand prior to the play and that she did not want to look weak around the other players. However, Erik rebuts her and explains that she acted too early. Konnikova explains that the most crucial mistake she made, outside of the poor strategy which Erik said is the easiest part, was that she did not have any good reason for her decisions. Erik advises her to take a few seconds of reflection before every action and to stop and take a breath to think through her options whenever she plays.

Maria compares Erik to that of a dragonfly in the wild. She says, "he just watches quietly—and then changes his hunting approach based on what he's observed.." Konnikova tells the story of how Erik won the title in the European Poker Tour Grand Final Super High Roller champion back in 2015. She recalls how Erik was at a disadvantage card-wise but was calm and collected and observed the slightest of motions from his opponent. In contrast to being described as a dragonfly, Erik says that he identifies himself more as a part of a jazz band. He explains that in a jazz band, you're trying to play "connected and in sync with the rest of the players." He stresses how in this context and in this comparison, you had to be a free thinker.

The chapter ends with Konnikova sharing how she was approached by a magazine to write an article. According to her, the magazine has contacted her before, but she never took them on their offers because of the low pay for the effort required. When they offered her the assignment, she said that she was not really doing freelance work at the time. Here, Maria does not reject them outright but "stay[s] in the hand to see what will happen." After their exchange, she was able to increase the rate that was originally offered to her. She ends by saying "I've won the hand and extracted more value than I ever thought I could from it."

6. A Man's World

The next chapter is entitled *A Man's World* in the winter of 2016. We find the author in her first live tournament where she finds actors, directors, famous athletes, and poker celebrities. Konnikova explains that she had thought that she would be going to her first live tourney as an observer, but Erik set her up to be one of the event's participants. "Hey, it'll be fun. Jamie is playing, too" Erik says to Konnikova. Jamie is Erik's daughter. Erik explains that the poker scene is a particularly "harsh environment for women". They had to work twice as hard to survive in the poker scene, which Konnikova writes, is made up of almost 97% male. But the female players who are serious with their poker game tended to be in a class of their own, according to Erik.

Konnikova describes the room: the crowd may be full of women but most of the people sitting at the tables were men. She realizes at this point that a lot of her aggressive playing style prior to the live tourney was because of social conditioning. "Over the years, I've learned that it doesn't pay to be aggressive while female," she explains. Konnikova highlights this point by citing a Harvard study, where it was found that women were more likely to be penalized for asking for more money in any given negotiation.

We are then taken to her first table, where she recalls "is nothing like playing online." Although it isn't, Konnikova is slowly able to "doggy-paddle" and remembers to "pause before every decision" this time around. After a few hours of playing, she finds that she's actually having fun. Because of her newfound feeling,

Maria opts to bet big in one of her hands and unfortunately loses, even with a halfway decent hand. She thinks to herself, "I can't possibly keep losing" but quickly rebuts that this was a gambler's fallacy or the faulty idea that probability had a memory. She underscores that if anyone wants to be a competent player, he or she must acknowledge that no one is "due" for good cards or good karma.

Afterwards, the author discusses a psychology concept first introduced by Julian Rotter in 1966 termed the *locus of control*. This is asking the question of: when something happens in the external environment, is it because of our own actions or skills (internal) or is it because of some outside factor (external). The author relates this concept to her current situation, by saying that people who focused more on what they could control proved to be more successful in life. She says that her internal locus of control was what got her to the table.

Maria manages to stay in the game for just over three hours. She describes a particular encounter in her game where an aggressive hedge fund "guy" re-raised or challenges her at the table. She does not fold and feels that she was being pushed around by the guy, so she decides to hold her ground. Her fellow tablemates chime in and tell her that she must not let herself be pushed around and should call his "bluff." Although she knew better not to challenge him, she did so. Unfortunately, the hedge fund guy had the better hand and Maria's first live poker tournament came to an end.

The chapter ends with Maria talking to her husband after her defeat. He advises for her to go to sleep, reasoning that she had always told him that everything looked better in the morning. Maria follows her husband's wisdom, takes her laptop, and makes her way back home. She proclaims that while she "may not be ready yet...I'll be damned if I'm going to admit defeat."

7. No Bad Beats

The next chapter is entitled *No Bad Beats*, set in Las Vegas in the winter of 2017. The author describes her trip on the way to Las Vegas, which she says is a place that "shouldn't exist" for the "incongruity" it has. At one point, she describes that you'll see buildings and suddenly be met with nature. She arrives at the Las Vegas airport and recounts how reality and fiction are blurred, with each passenger immediately met with slot machines upon exiting the airport's gate. The author explains that Vegas is not your ordinary place of casinos, as Vegas itself is "designed to capture your attention and make itself look like the world in its entirety." Further accentuating Vegas' uniqueness, Erik tells Maria that they would be visiting American magician Teller's house (from Penn and Teller). He tells her that it's going to be destroyed by a tank. Konnikova ends the story of her arrival at Vegas by concluding that in Vegas, "games and life, fantasy and fact, have become so fused.... it's no longer quite possible to tell one from the other."

After this, we find Maria trying out for small tournaments and once again learning new terms such as *bankroll:* the amount of money you possess to devote to poker. She enters the $40 tournaments to start with, and finds out that early in her career, she still can't play the $140 games without a large enough bankroll. The author explains that poker is an unforgiving game, where if you risk "too big," any player could find themselves broke. Konnikova pays respect to Erik in this regard, complimenting his ability to stay calm in the worst of times.

Erik and Maria then talk about which tournament she would join while in Vegas. They pick the Golden Nugget. After which, Erik tells her that she might be able to make The Ladies Event in the WSOP, which makes Maria uneasy. She says that while she understood his intention to separate women into a separate pool, having to join such an event felt demoralizing. She makes two promises: first was that she would stick with her endeavor and master the game; second, if she was going to become known in the game, she wanted to be known as a good poker player, not a good female poker player. She holds that she did not want any modifiers to apply.

The next scene has Maria almost getting her first tournament cash. This ends in her unfortunately busting out and she describes feeling devastated. Erik emphasizes that "bad beats" were a bad mental habit to have in the sport and urges her not to dwell on them as they did not help her become a better player whatsoever. This exchange sparks a discussion from the author about how our framing of something affects not just our emotional state. She says that the "words we select.... are a mirror to our thinking." Moreover, she says that there is no such thing as objective reality because everytime we experience something, we interpret it for ourselves.

She continues talking about "bad beats" and how in choosing to dwell in our errors or misfortunes, we fail to see the things or actions that we could do to overcome them. She stresses that if one thinks of himself as an "almost-victor", it will eventually drain you as you continually paint yourself as a victim. The author says that bad beats such as having a bad table draw could force you to play well. Bad beats force you to "play the best version of your game." She ends the chapter by doubling down on her sentiments about bad beats by saying that wallowing in them only focuses your mind on something you can't control, rather than something you can, which is the decision.

8. Texting Your Way out of Millions

The next chapter is entitled *Texting Your Way out of Millions*, in Las Vegas, winter, 2017. In this chapter, the author talks once again about Vegas. She describes it as the "true America" and the poker table as the "American dream". She makes these comparisons with how anyone from any walk of life could go to Vegas and try their hand in the sport. One example she shares is one of the players in the tournament who came from rural West Virginia where the poverty rate is above 20%. He only had his mother in his life and had a father that was an alcoholic, who repeatedly found himself in jail. The player experienced homelessness and was told by many that he would "never

amount to anything." And yet, the author shares that the player is now worth millions and is considered one of the best poker players in the world. Konnikova underscores her point about poker being the American dream, explaining that in the sport, "everyone is allowed." She says that no one would turn you away if you weren't from the right school or had the right connections. You just had to be skillful enough to earn the right to play.

In the next scene, we have Maria and Erik talking about paying attention. Maria talks about how Erik really was the "bassist" as he was able to hold everything together and adjust to balance out all the other instruments or players in each game. Erik tells Maria to observe and watch a player named Andrew Lichtenberger or more commonly known as "Chewy". He says that in terms of focus, he is one of the best there is. Maria explains that Chewy is a rare exception in the world of professional poker because he was always present and watchful. This was in stark contrast to most elite players which were always on their phones, texting, scrolling through sports scores, making bets, and following hands only when they were involved.

Maria continues her discussion on the importance of paying attention. She stresses that attention is a "powerful mitigator to overconfidence" because it forces you to always reevaluate and reassess what you knew and the game plan you had. She added that paying attention is also one of the best ways to minimize the window of negative variance. Maria explains that in an age of distraction and never-ending connectivity, paying attention allows us to catch the signals that tell us to swerve before we run into bad beats. Without attention, these signals would easily be missed

The chapter ends with Maria talking about how Chewy approached losing. She contrasts Chewy's approach with that of Dan Harrington's. For Harrington, losing was an essential part of learning how to win. For Chewy, it was a more cosmic occurrence that he saw as part of a larger pattern or a bigger picture. He explains this by saying that maybe at an instance of losing "....we weren't meant to win that hand because some other stream of events had to transpire for us to be successful."

9. Storytelling Business

The next chapter of the book is entitled A *Storytelling Business*, set in Las Vegas, last March 2017. In this chapter, Erik tells Maria that she had to meet Phil Galfond, one of the best players and who was described to be "likely the single best poker teacher in the world." While Konnikova was initially hesitant to meet him, her apprehensions quickly disappeared as she discovered that Galfond was one of the most affable and friendliest people she has ever encountered. He is the owner of the training site, Run It Once, that Erik asked Maria to sign up for.

In their first meeting, Phil tells Maria that the first and most crucial thing she needs to know is that poker is storytelling. He tells her that the game is a narrative puzzle, where it's the player's job to put the pieces together. In poker, according to Phil, you're both a detective and a storyteller. Therefore, it's your job to figure out what the actions of your opponent's mean, and at the same time, what they don't mean as well. He emphasizes further that while you must be aware of other players, you also need to take note of yourself as a subject of the same exact process. Everything that you think about regarding others can be applied to your own actions just the same, which Phil says is something that most players often forget.

The discussion is expounded further. As the storyteller of the narrative, it is essential that you understand what motivates each of the characters or players in the game. Why do they do what they're doing, he says. Searching for narrative cohesiveness, Phil underscores is key. He goes so far as to say that even terrible players make questionable moves for a reason, and it is your job as the storyteller to figure out why. He tells Maria that she shouldn't judge or them. Rather, she must figure out the reasons why they made such and such plays despite how awful they may be. Phil also stresses the importance of knowing the why. He urges further that she should never do anything, no matter how small, without asking precisely why she was going to do it.

Maria agrees. She reflects about how we would never take a moment to ask why a certain person makes a decision we don't necessarily agree with. Maria continues to ask how much time could have been saved if we learned to ask why they acted the way they did, rather than judge and make presumptions about them. Phil's last piece of wisdom for Maria is for her to take all that they talked about, go out there, and apply it all.

The next part of the chapter has Maria waking up early for her next tournament: a 10 AM game at Planet Hollywood. She recounts how she has been slowly getting more familiar with the fast pace of having daily tourneys and tries to follow the lessons she's learned even with the time constraints. In one of the games, she finds herself as the table chip leader. It is in this junction that one of the players remaining at the table suggests that they do a *chop*, meaning they would divide the remaining pot amongst themselves. He tells her that she'll get more money, especially now that she's in a position of power. However, Maria refuses and continues to play. Their table starts to dwindle, and she eventually wins her first live tournament, with winnings of around $900. Konnikova enjoys this moment and says that beyond the cash she won, the win was crucial for her confidence. It made her feel like all the hours she spent studying were showing signs of paying off.

Before they left for Vegas, Erik and Maria planned out her next few months. In a month and a half, the European Poker Tour, she says, would be holding its annual event in Monte Carlo. Erik tells her that it wouldn't be a bad idea for her to go, taking this statement from Erik as a rare point of direction from her poker coach.

The last part of the chapter shows a scene of Maria back from Vegas, with her husband at home. Konnikova had just gotten off the phone with a speaking agency and found her husband observing her quietly. She shares that it was her first time turning down a speaking engagement in her whole career, reasoning out to the agency that she was worth more than what they had offered to her. Maria's husband tells her in admiration, "you take much less shit from people than you used to...that's really good." The chapter ends here.

10.   The Gambler and the Nerd

The next chapter is entitled *The Gambler and the Nerd*, where we find Maria now in Monte Carlo in April 2017. The author tells the reader that everything else in her poker journey had been nothing but batting practice. All the daily tournaments in Vegas were small-time local games. Being in Monte Carlo meant that she was now participating in an "international baller". The chapter starts with the author arriving in the Mediterranean through a helicopter ride. She describes Monte Carlo as a place for the rich, where having €1-2 million in other places would be admired, but in this particular place you would be pitied.

The author shares the story of how John von Neumann, the aforementioned inspiration of Konnikova for starting her project, had been in Monte Carlo. John had devised a statistical system, she says, that would enable him to win the roulette table. Unfortunately, this doesn't pan out and he ends up flat broke in the casino. There he meets Klari, whom he shares his story with. Maria reveals that while von Neumann's system did not work in Monte Carlo, it would eventually give way to some of the most important applied mathematics of the time. His time there would also be where he would meet his eventual wife—Klari.

In the next part of this chapter, Maria arrives early for her first event—the €1,100 National Championship. On the way to find Erik, Maria recounts finding comedian Kevin Hart with another poker player. The author introduces us to the concept of a *prop bet*, which are "bets on a specific proposition." Hart and the poker player were currently in the middle of a prop bet themselves, with the poker player having to complete 105 push-ups in under 22 minutes in the middle of his $100k tournament. He was able to do so, with the timer ending at 21:52.

By 2 AM, Maria shares her happiness that she had made day 2. This meant that she was officially in the money. She explains that with the structure of the tournament, the first day plays until 12% of the field remains. After this, everyone is guaranteed a minimum cash amount. Soon after, however, Maria busts the following day as the 193rd. 293 people were able to survive to reach the second day, and Maria proudly declares that she was one of them.

The next part finds Erik explaining to Maria that her cash rate was "too much," which was something that surprised her. Erik says that the math makes it so the money is concentrated up top, which meant that the only people who made money were the participants who made the final table. Erik says to Maria that she needs to be playing, not for the minimum cash, but play to win. Maria realizes that Erik was right, every single time she would play not to reach the final table but to merely hold on to the money...and then bust right after. Erik tells her that he would "rather you cash less but go deeper."

The author subsequently talks about how she was experiencing firsthand the learning trajectory she tried to model so often in the lab, in relation to Erik's latest piece of advice. She says, "the more you learn, the harder it gets....because the flaws you wouldn't even think of looking at before are now visible and need to be addressed." She starts to ask herself if she also went for the minimum cash in her life decisions, enquiring if she goes with the safe thing rather than taking more risk for the more attractive but still uncertain choice.

The chapter ends with Erik and Maria planning for her to take smaller events to see how everything coalesced. Erik emphasizes that she should take her time, because if she was really looking to go for it, she had to assess where she was at with her game. He tells her that she shouldn't hold herself to an arbitrary deadline. Maria, in her head, responds that she has never missed a deadline and did not intend to start now.

11. The Art of the Tell

The next chapter is called *The Art of the Tell*, set in New York, in May 2017. This section focuses on the poker "tell" or reading the well-known act of poker players reading their opponents' faces, movements, or mannerisms to gain an advantage. This section starts off with Maria playing a poker game and a new player joining their table. The new player is wearing a white ribbed tank top and his biceps were covered in tattoos. Konnikova says that she knew just the type, concluding from her prior experiences that he would be an aggressive player. Unfortunately, her analysis would fall flat as she was put in a position where she had a 70% chance of losing. Luckily for her, she was saved by a miracle card and the new player left two hands later. She realizes that she made a mistake because she wasn't using *tells* in reading the new player. Rather, she was using her implicit biases. Maria holds that if she were going to succeed, she would have to become better at the thing she thought she was so good at, dealing with people.

Maria discusses how human brains are wired to constantly make sense of the environment, making guesses at what would happen next. This applied to people, wherein she further explained that we tend to make "thin-slice judgments of people" which usually turned out to be false. She recounts a poker player she had played with, an old Russian that she helped translate English for, who turned out to have "played her" through her kindness. She realizes that he probably knew English and just tried to get her on his side. Furthermore, Konnikova explains that people are adept at making excuses for ourselves and making up explanations for why we are still as good as we thought, even if this is not really the case.

The next section of the chapter, the author introduces is to Michael Slepian. He worked on the psychology of thin slice-judgments and in a series of three studies, he and his colleagues studied how people reacted to particular poker hands. Maria describes the results as curious: with one group that saw hands, the participants reacted normally; with the group that saw the cards and the faces of the player, their judgments dropped below average levels. Maria explains that faces may give more false information than we thought. The author finds that one must be more attuned to pay attention, as her coach Erik has continually preached throughout the book. Maria ends the chapter by vowing that in the next two months, she would look less at the souls or faces of her opponents and focus more on their hands/cards. She stresses that she would pay attention more to every movement that happens in the game, be it shuffles, bets, calls, checks, or raises.

12.   Reading Myself

Moving on to the next chapter, we find the section called *Reading Myself*, set in New York, in 2017 from May to June. We are introduced in this chapter to former psychologist turned professional poker player Blake Eastman. His work, Beyond Tells, is the central talking point in the chapter. It is considered the largest ever study of poker players in the poker table. The two of them meet to talk about his study. Eastman, according to the author, disliked the word "tells" because it gave a too simplistic perspective of what his study was all about. He says that tells are not just one gesture or movement or act, they are repeatable patterns or behaviors that are taken as a whole.

According to Eastman and his study, a large amount of information could be grasped from one's gestures. He says that "confident people move[d] from point A to point B quickly." Maria elaborates and says that if you look at enough hands over a long amount of time, you start to develop a sense of patterns that could give you meaningful information. She explains that if you had *aces*, for example, she would know exactly what to do. But if she received a more awkward hand, like a *seven-nine*, she would be less predictable. Here, she realizes that whatever act she may do on the poker table, she may have been inadvertently communicating her very own thought process to the other players.

She further mentions that the most telling moment in each poker game is at the very beginning, where players first check their hole cards. How they check their cards and what they do immediately after, according to Konnikova, could be the most honest actions a player will have during the entire hand. Aside from this, she also discusses the concept of concealment, or the act by which players actively try to hide what they think are "telling behaviors". Eastman explains to her that finding out how other players concealed could be another step to determine exactly what they may be concealing.

After their first meeting, Eastman agrees to watch Konnikova play poker to better gauge what kind of information she gave off to other players. In summary, he found that Maria 1) checked her cards too many times, 2) put her cards on the cards, and 3) double-checked her hole cards repeatedly. All of these were things that Eastman suggested for her not to do anymore because they gave too much information. To replace these, he said that she should be more consistent not in her motions, but in her execution. "Stop, think about what you want to do, and execute," Eastman said.

With her time with Eastman, the author shares that she has learned to tell the difference between one's own faulty intuitions and real data, to better understand how to exploit this information, and to know if you yourself are being exploited. Konnikova ends the chapter by saying that in her studies about tells and reads, she missed a crucial step. She underscores that the first person you had to profile psychologically, was not others, but yourself.

13.   Full Tilt

The next chapter in the book is entitled *Full Tilt,* where we find Maria in Las Vegas, in June to July 2017. In this chapter, we find Maria in the Colossus. This was her first World Series Event, which cost $565 to buy in and is considered one of the most affordable of the WSOP bracelet events. Maria recounts her experience on the way to the event, how she got lost and did not know her way around, as well as her encounter with the venue's numerous bazaars and sellers that lined up in between her and the poker tournament.

After three days, Maria's expenses have ballooned from $565 to $2,825. She was able to quickly reverse her fortune and achieve her very first official WSOP cash: placing 237th for $2,247. She placed 237th in a pool of over 2,000 participants. With two weeks passing, her final tally is summarised as follows: $11,810 in entry money and $5,748 in cashes, for a net loss of $6,062. Even with the net loss, Erik reassures her that it is no easy feat to have earned her first three cases in her first ever WSOP.

In this chapter, Maria questions whether she was ready for the Main Event - the main destination in her project to begin with. She discusses the *planning fallacy*, where humans tend to be overly optimistic about mapping out timelines and goals, as we always looked at the best case scenario and never the realistic one. While she has apprehensions about whether she is ready for the tourney or not, Maria chooses to stick with her plan. This is despite Erik's advice for her to reassess and take things slowly. He had told her that if the book were the only reason for her to compete at the moment, she could just postpone. But Maria, furthering her explanation, discusses the *status quo bias* and how we tend to continue with our actions despite new information. She decides to move forward with her plan because it would be a hit to her reputation and be a demonstration of failure.

In this part of the book, Maria talks in a more retrospective and hindsight view of the things that happened. She says that one of the most important lessons in poker strategy was self-assessment, knowing what not to do, letting go. Maria cites an example to illustrate this point: when we start a "promising job" only to be left behind on promotions but still maintaining that the job is great. She tells the reader that we must be "willing to read the signs and let it go."

Her doubt with the Main Event continues as she shares that on the morning of the tournament, she had a chance to call it off. She shares that Erik has never forced her to play an event and did not want her to. He would always say, according to Konnikova, that she should "see how you feel in the morning". However, Maria still moves forward with her plan.

In the next few scenes, we now find Maria playing in the Main Event tournament. During the second day, she had already lost a good amount of chips: from 50,000, down to 29,500. Erik encourages her and reassures her that it was great for her to even reach the second day. At this time, Maria harkens back to the first chapter of the book, where she was in the bathroom, migraine and all. She tells Erik that she is "Hanging in there" while still facing much difficulty at that moment. Unfortunately, Maria ends up busting at the tournament because of her rash decision making. She recalls that she couldn't even blame her migraine because "the only culprit here [was] me."

We are then introduced to Jared Tendler, who would be Maria's mental game coach. After her loss in the Main, she is met by Tendler to help her with what happened. Tendler emphasizes that Maria should stop "hoping" to do better next year and remove the word "hope" in her system altogether. He stresses that what she should be to "just do". Maria realizes that she should not have played in the Main. That decision of her to play was based on "hope", when it should have been based on "doing." She says she knew that she still had a lot more to accomplish before she would be ready for such an event, which is why she shouldn't have joined in the first place.

The next part of the chapter talks about the concept of *tilt*. Tilt is when you let your emotions, incidental emotions not integral to your decision process, affect your decision making. Maria explains that emotions are not all bad when it comes to decision making. They could serve to be useful markers for making the correct choice. However, when these emotions are not integral to the decision process, tilt can make you revert to your "worst self". Maria and Tendler then work on identifying these emotions, analyzing their cause, and making them less influential in one's decision making. Jared gives Maria an assignment to map out her emotional process so they could find ways to solve each problem. She finds out that she reacts to other players who instruct her on what to do, hit on her, or demean her by calling her "little girl". The situations that spark her emotions, she finds, are the ones where she feels as if her own agency as a person is being compromised. When they find out these triggers, she devises a plan of wearing noise-cancelling headphones, to anticipate the emotions and subsequently solve the problem.

Ending the discussion of her *tilt*, Maria reveals that the root of her emotions stems from a fear of being a fraud. She recounts a story in kindergarten when they had just moved to the US. She was given a name tag that wasn't hers and because she couldn't speak English, she could only cry out. "That's not me, I want to scream." In her current situation, she fears being a fraud who "doesn't deserve to be playing..." Maria explains that she has a constant anxiety of letting people down. This is countered by Jared, wherein he tells her that she must overcome her fear because she was "instinctively cowering to future Maria's power." He tells her that while she may be wrong in the actions she intended to do, being afraid of her future self was the bigger mistake.

Thereafter, they start implementing the lessons they learned, and Maria starts a balanced approach to her training. She recharges by going home to her husband, but also maintains a plan so she doesn't go three weeks without playing. She begins to be more comfortable, meet new friends, make acquaintances. Soon after, she reached second place in her first final table of an international event at PokerStars in Dublin. She takes another second place soon after back in Las Vegas, with her biggest score to date at almost $6,000. She even agreed to "chop" during another poker game, because she realized that it was the objectively better decision.

The chapter ends with Maria looking ahead to her next event, the PokerStars Caribbean Adventure or the PCA. The PCA, she says, is one of the oldest live poker tour stops in the world, going on now for over thirteen years.

14.   The Glory Days

The next chapter is entitled *The Glory Days*, where we find Maria in the Bahamas in January 2019 for the PCA. The first part of the chapter talks about Konnikova dealing with the lack of sleep. She consults fellow poker players about what remedies they used to fall asleep better, with some suggesting caffeine pills, drugs, etc. However, the main plot in this chapter is when Maria starts to play in the PCA itself. Maria becomes one of the last eight players in the international tournament and is now at the final table. The author recalls how she had felt like everyone deserved to be at the final table, but her. The chapter recounts her ups and downs in the round, where at the beginning she had lost a big chunk of her chips from a wrong decision in her hand. She is met at that point with encouragement from Erik to take it one hand at a time. Maria picks her spots and maintains her mental discipline during the final stretches of the game. One by one, her tablemates leave the final table until she eventually becomes the last person sitting. She wins. She wins $84,600, after beating her heads-up opponent Alexander Ziskin. She reveals that she becomes the 2018 PCA National Champion.

The next part of the chapter, we find that Maria Konnikova feels apprehensive about ending her story at the point of her victory. She tells the readers that it felt "too elegant. Too clean." She starts to question whether her win was in fact because of her skill or due to the goddess of luck. She asks, "how will I ever know: Am I really good—or did I just get lucky?"

15.   The Heart of the Gambling Beast

The Heart of the Gambling Beast is the second to the last chapter of the book, set in Macau, in March of 2018. We find Maria fresh off her victory from the PCA and she shares that her story is beloved by the poker world

. "From nothing to champion," she says, and her popularity grew as she was even offered by PokerStars, the host of the PCA, with a formal sponsorship as one of their professional players in their roster. However, even with her sweet victory, Maria is adamant that she would not become or be considered a one-hit wonder. She seeks to answer the question of whether she was really more than just a "fraud who has luckboxed into an international title."

In the next scene, Maria chooses to go to Macau to try her hand once again in the game and try to answer the question raised above. Macau, according to Konnikova, is Vegas but bigger and weirder. She says that "Macau is a shrine to the goddess of chance." She goes to Macau to take part in the Asia Pacific Poker Tour or APPT. In between her tournament during the APPT, Konnikova discusses with Ike Haxton, one of the most logical minds in poker, with Erik, regarding the concept of superstition. She's surprised to find out that even with the mathematical approach that Ike takes, he purposefully cultivates superstition. According to Ike, while he does not personally believe in superstitions, he still does so because of an understanding that his "mind is going to make these associations no matter what." In response, Erik is straightforward in his rejection of delusion or superstition as he feels that it only "cultivates the wrong mindset."

After this discussion, Konnikova reveals that in the ten or more days that she spends in Macau, she was able to reach not one, but two final tables. Although she was not able to attain another championship, she does add a second-place finish to her resume. This was worth almost $60,000. She says that she has "gotten what she came for." According to Maria, Macau would be her last tournament for some time because, Maria shares, that she was able to subsequently cash in at her first ever Main. She relates although she didn't reach the final table, in this moment, she feels that she hasn't let Erik down after all. After two weeks, Maria says that she had gone to the European Poker Tour (EPT) where she notched her best ever EPT finish at 34th place out of 1,500 entries. This was worth €9,200

When the Global Poker Index (GPI) awards were announced, Maria Konnikova was named a finalist for the Breakout Player of the Year. Even with all the accolades, the author explains that she does experience a decline in her career. In the summer of 2019, she loses money compared to her $100,000 earnings from the year before. She reassures the reader however that she is currently in the right direction. These days, she says that she now has the tools to understand such moments of decline, not panic, analyze, study, and move on to try and improve. Although her poker career was not good in 2019, her family experienced much better luck at the time. Her mother was able to find a new profession in teaching kids how to code and her husband was able to start his new business. The chapter ends with yet another encounter of Maria's with her grandmother, where her elder still is not agreeable to her granddaughter's decision to play the game. She merely accepts that "some things never change, no matter how much I accomplish."

16.   The Lucid Fallacy

The last chapter of the book is entitled *The Lucid Fallacy*, in Las Vegas, last June 2019. The chapter starts with Maria losing both her eyesight and her hearing. She falls into the floor and focuses on one thing: to try and stay conscious. It turned out that Maria had come from a long night of playing poker and she couldn't sleep in after her games with the fear of her chips slowly losing their height. After a few moments, her husband comes to assist her. Soon we find out that it was caused by an anomalous type of her usual migraines, and a *vasovagal event* or a sudden drop in her heart rate and blood pressure. They originally feared that it was a stroke. While it wasn't the case, her experience still "wasn't good."

The doctor, during her appointment, was surprised that she was able to stay awake during her whole ordeal. Maria explains her astonishment at the fact that she was able to stay calm during this situation. According to Konnikova, she couldn't believe that she was able to accept what was happening and form a plan. She observes that this was a vastly different "me" from the "me" two years prior.

In the last parts of the book, Maria discusses how in some ways poker tends to be a poor substitute for life. She relates her experience in losing her senses in the bathroom where she ended up in the emergency room, which compared to merely busting out in a tournament, was far different. She makes it clear here however, that no one was asking for poker to be equated with life. It would be presumptuous to believe it was possible, she says. We merely want to understand both.

She ends the book by emphasizing that "nothing is all skill. Life is life, luck will always be a factor." She explains that "all we can do is mitigate the damage" from the things that we cannot control. And here is where Konnikova responds to the mystery of her book's title *The Biggest Bluff*. What is it? According to her, it is that "skill can ever be enough". She highlights that it is our hope that when we're faced with things we can't control, when luck is stacked against us, when we don't know if we can manage life, "we must convince ourselves that we can." She ends, "that in the end, our skill will be enough to carry the day. Because it has to be."

CPSIA information can be obtained
at www.ICGtesting.com
Printed in the USA
BVHW092248180822
644988BV00008B/128

9 798695 009040